Collecting the Light

University of Central Florida
Contemporary Poetry Series

Collecting the Light

Poems by

Markham Johnson

University Press of Florida
Gainesville / Tallahassee / Tampa / Boca Raton
Pensacola / Orlando / Miami / Jacksonville

Library of Congress Cataloging-in-Publication Data

Johnson, Markham.
Collecting the light/Markham Johnson.
p. cm.—(University of Central Florida contemporary poetry series)
ISBN 0-8130-1229-5.—ISBN 0-8130-1230-9 (paper)
I. Title. II. Series: Contemporary poetry series (Orlando, Fla.)
PS3560.0381406 1993
811'.54dc—20 93-1389

"Voices" first appeared in the *Cimarron Review* and is reprinted here with the permission of the Board of Regents for Oklahoma State University, holders of the copyright.

The University Press of Florida is the scholarly publishing agency for the State University System of Florida, comprised of Florida A & M University, Florida Atlantic University, Florida International University, Florida State University, University of Central Florida, University of Florida, University of North Florida, University of South Florida, and University of West Florida.

University Press of Florida
15 Northwest 15th Street
Gainesville, FL 32611

Acknowledgments

Thanks are due to the following magazines in which these poems first appeared:

Calliope: "Carp and Drum," originally entitled "Getting Over"
Cimarron Review: "Voices"
Great River Review: "The All-Night Diner"
Louisville Review: "Iowa Winter"
Nimrod: "On the Road"
Passages North: "Butchers"
Pennsylvania Review: "Starlings, Grackles, Redwings"
Sonora Review: "Harvest"
Spitball: The Literary Baseball Magazine: "Obsession: Elegy for Roger Maris and Georgia O'Keeffe"
Visions: "Collecting the Light"

"Butchers" appeared in the anthology, *Passages North Anthology: A Decade of Good Writing*, edited by Elinor Benedict (1990).

The following poems first appeared in the chapbook *Starlings, Grackles, Redwings*, published by *South Florida Poetry Review:* "Harvest," "Iowa Winter," "Butchers," "Desire," "Starlings," "The Legend of Kingman Boulevard, After Hours," "On the Road," "Skating By Ice House Light," "Starlings, Grackles, Redwings," "This Miracle Was Meant for Her Alone" (originally entitled "Audience"), "On Hearing My Grandmother's House Will Be Sold," "Collecting the Light."

Special thanks to Chris Seid, Tom Tomshany, Ruth Doty, Mark Doty, Jack Myers, and Roger Weingarten for their support, insight, and general good will.

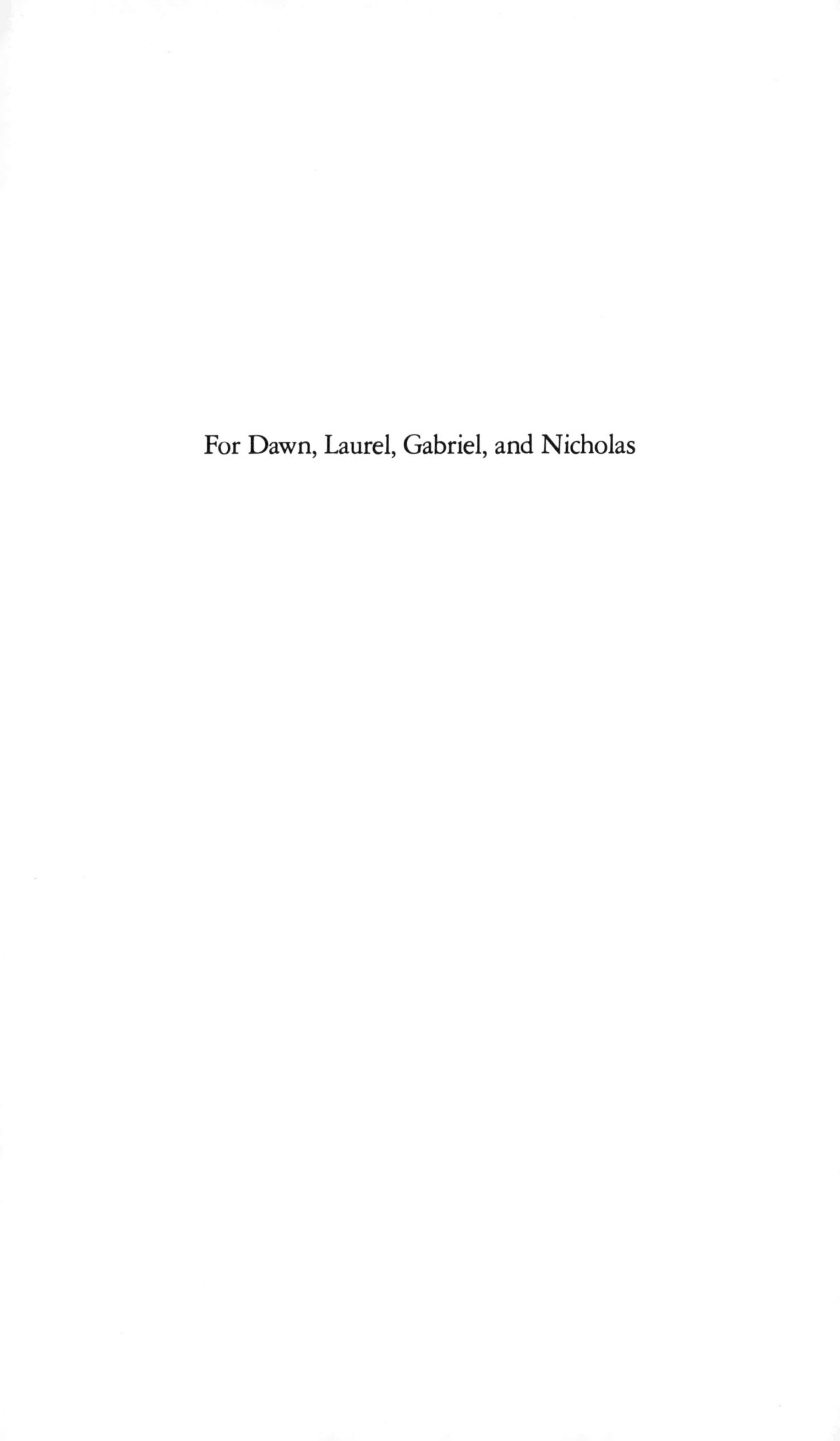

For Dawn, Laurel, Gabriel, and Nicholas

CONTENTS

III

Harvest

Over these acres of corn picked clean,
The same stars of summer circle through fall,
Awake all night, while we have passed inside
To ferry our children through sleep.

Coming home tonight, I find the field I have driven by
All summer, with the deep fog of morning
Rising through green stalks, is gone.
The harvester has taken it while I was away.

Some night our children will explain these things
To themselves; some night when we lie alone again,
Under the stars picked clean, waiting
For the fog to rise out of the dust of our hair.

Part
I

My Grandmother Returns from the Graveyard of Dogs, and Horses, and Plows

For two days we thought she might never return,
slipping her knotted fingers into the furred pockets
of the astral world. But now, Grandmother wakes
from the machined breath of intensive care,
where at midnight the comotose lift completely clear
of their roll-away bodies—a fantastic trick.

She was walking the halls, she tells us,
listening for her dogs wandering Highway 66,
the cows, straying from their delicate dreams,
the burn patients moaning like sheep at sunset.

Maybe she was searching the pediatrics ward
for 1959, as if, at eighty-five, she'd arrived
at that year she slept beside my hospital bed,
each night of the month of December, a wall
of translucent vinyl, slipped between us, like death
lisping his S's of pure oxygen, patting
the heads of children up and down the hall.

No, its just the back pasture she has lost.
The horses have been out all night
dripping with rain. She crawls inside
her yellow raincoat, the one she wears
in every weather, with her favorite flashlight
weaving, at her feet, the body's tattered light.

At the end of the gravel drive, she finds the horses,
Molly, Susie, and Liberty Bell, asleep on their feet,
swaying among the litter of old harrows and bailers,
as if something heavy had crawled out of their hides.
They are so old, she doesn't even wake them,
anymore, rubbing her light slowly over their sides.

Finally, she returns to us, years later,
from the bramble of blackberries ringing
the graveyard of dogs and horses and plows.
By the tool shed, we find her
tapping the last damp earth from her shovel.

Butchers

Hooting from milk crates, outside
the back door, the butchers
with scarlet aprons like tongues
between their knees,
on break from the tedium of hacking
meat from bone, play mumblety-peg
with cleavers in the high weeds.

After surgery for a tumor pressing
for years on the brain,
my grandfather told stories
of family never spoken of before,
his father and five uncles, butchers
in the same shop on Cheyenne,
swinging their knives to the creak
of swinging meat.

Each with his chopping block and rhythm,
the 3/4 time of German stock,
for years raising axes overhead.
"I remember how those cows went down
splaylegged," he says, "skin stripped down
like a glove." And inside
the ambling track of veins mapping
the simple animal inconsistencies.
When he is gone another thirty years
will be forgotten: my grandfather,
with hands that laid hold of rusted machines,
tearing metal from metal,
in the screech of lugs worn threadbare,
at eighty laying hold of me like I was ten.

And what is forgotten like dirt
folded under, like sleep laid over
the bones? Five uncles and a father
in their second-generation-immigrant
trade, and their father who whipped
the welterweight champ in Kansas City.
In Sand Springs, the grocery that burned
where only oil, like water,
seeped out of the ground.

Here in this small town where the meat market
and VFW Hall are all that remain,
like old soldiers gathering
each Thursday night for sixty years,
Grandfather dozes on the screened porch
afraid only of dying in an empty room,
no starlings cackling an hour before dawn,
no brothers laughing, kicking stones
on the short walk home.
Starched white aprons,
and the blood spray over all.

On Hearing My Grandmother's House Will Be Sold

1.
In the dusty slippers of autumn, my mother and aunt
        crawl back forty years
through newspaper cutouts, wedding veils, and filed
        in Webster's under *love*,
the last purpled flecks of summer's high school corsage,
        to finally arrive
at seventeen, in the same unfinished attic of today.
        From their mother's last
garden they rise, from columbine latticing a rough
        hedge of tomatoes—
the last green knotted thumbs of September, tucked
        in baskets, and stacked
in the attic, among remnants of her world: porcelain
        remains of china dolls,
an armoire of yellowed camisoles, and collected on yearly
        calendars, Ruth's daily reminders
to herself—phone numbers of the dead, and a shopping list
        of astral theory,
scattered quotations of Madame Blavatsky and Annie Besant.

2.
In my grandmother's new room at the nursing home,
        each drawer of her dresser
is cocked open, spilling black and whites and sixties polaroids,
        like a busted seam
in the garden of total recall: her photographs, endless
        fruits of September—
scattered over every square of linoleum, hugging blankets,
        slipped under pillows—
old wishes still waiting to be fulfilled. She whispers,
        "the crazy woman next door

stole my favorite pictures, but I took them back
while she was asleep,"
and collected on the bed, among Johnsons and Rushs
and Tomshanys, I find
whole families I do not recognize, as if Grandma had returned
with a sack of new
memories, from long nights wandering the astral plane.

3.
At lunch, she retells my favorite story, of a summer
we met in Munich,
in her tourist hotel. But this time, we are in Jerusalem,
long after dark.
She has been awake for hours, the black flies humming
to the distant mutter
of cannon fire over Galilee. Alone, she wanders
the Arab Quarter,
the Temple Mount, Damascus Gate, until she finds me again,
after four years,
playing cards on the Via Dolorosa, in a smoky cafe.
Maybe it really happened that way.
Today I would like to recall, for both of us, everything
she explained to me
at sixteen, an age when I believed nothing yet was worth
remembering.
As I am leaving I whisper, "Grandma, next time I will see you
in Bombay."
"India," she says, "Yes, I have that picture somewhere. We have
already met in Bombay."

Translating Voices into Flight

Sometimes, I still hear the clothesline hum
of Billy Winter's voice stretched
between two Libbey's pineapple cans,
a private telephone line flinging
our twelve year old epithets, up to the treehouse,
and high in the air, the way George,
my grandfather's childhood friend
could throw his voice—his cat singing
Irving Berlin, the couch barking
beneath him. "He was a terrible liar,"
Grandfather said, "you could only believe
his pillow's soft stutter early mornings
while George was still asleep in bed."

Years later, on his back, my grandfather
could tell no more stories,
the useless muscles of arms and legs
stained white with Parkinsons,
the great weight of his body returned
to the essential values of sinew and bone.
For those last months, the husky voices
of faded sunlight, of sleep rising
from toes and legs gone numb,
of the fallen arches of hardwood floors,
spread over him the way a newborn
hears everything, before
he has learned what not to listen for.

I imagine him turning a little on his side,
listening in on family in the next room.
When he closes his eyes, their words
become a flock of childhood magpies,
in a shocking Alabama snowfall,

smacking the plateglass kitchen window.
He wants to let them in, to fill
whole rooms with these ignorant birds,
to make a new life of words translated
into the knotted fibers of clothesline, into feathers,
into wings, into a common language of flight.

Where the Light Comes From

Each morning, my grandmother rises
to new songs waking from her piano—
"Blue Potato Rag," "The Box Top Polka"—
as if in her ninth decade, what remains
are the memories that shake loose
from her fingers.
She hums along to melodies no one else remembers,
from the summer she turned seventeen,
when she waited for someone to arrive,
to ask her to dance. She is letting go,
whole decades hauled off in sleep.
Her grandchildren peeled gently
from the photographs on her wall, finally
even her children have become distant fields.

Someday, Grandmother, we will all return
to seventeen, our collected decades,
like mail stacked unopened
on the kitchen table, the phone
ever ringing. We will have forgotten
everything, but the stars rolling through
the worn night. At twilight,
she leans over the piano, singing along
to "You're No Good, When You're Gone."
My grandfather has become her first
boyfriend, fresh from the alfalfa fields,
who has stopped in the middle
of her front lawn, surprised by the crop
of new stars sprung up over night,
wondering where the light comes from.

The Body's Perfect Details

Because we could not complete that first act
of dividing—one self from one self—

I remember, at five, when I burst
into the bedroom on a Sunday morning,

how you jerked up the grey wool skirt
to hide your belly's long red caesarean stain.

Now, at sixty, you've discovered nudes,
in life drawing class, caressing a warehouse

of Rodins, and like Da Vinci, tuck your fingers
under the skin, memorizing muscle fiber and bone.

Four decades you thought lost, scrubbed clean
with Lysol, in yellow rubber gloves,

until you imagined yourself transformed,
one sluffed layer of skin at a time. But this year,

when I return with my children, for Christmas,
I find a gallery of portraits and still-lifes

slapped on the walls, and in your sketch book,
a hundred charcoaled pages of naked men

and women. Mother, I want to say,
the body never learns to let go. Finally,

it all comes back to this: your artist's heart
kicking the blued, ecstatic ribs;

forty years of pictures cascading down
the corridors of slurred memory; and the way

you press your hands to the paper, repeating
the body's every imperfect detail.

On the Road

for Ben

On December nights as I lean over the balcony,
hearing Canada geese long before they pass,
I wonder, do they expect nothing,
after the first or second day, but flight—
the long feathered miles of half-frozen ponds,
cattails trailing glazed heads in the water.

Tonight, through the weariness of twenty-four hours
crossing the continent, my friends desire
only the slow waitresses. Married to the road
by now, passing Lake Champlain, our voices lost
in dense fog, we settle up with the ghosts
of dead grandfathers who do not recognize us,
sliding onto three empty stools
beside them a thousand miles from home.

It occurs to me, the dead carry on just this way,
a few gray memories cupping hands to their ears,
over the insistence of a noisy bar.
Itinerant travelers between isolate lives,
mostly they learn patience,
as no lover can reach them here,
only thin whispers through the party line of dreams.

Sometimes, they take the train for days,
drifting through sleep that wakes to nothing
less than roses set out on the kitchen table,
the empty cereal bowls of children;
a past so reasonable
they could almost crawl back inside,
through jumbled blankets,
through bedroom windows.

My grandfather is in the back room
shooting pool. I recognize the white mustache
he has carried past the grave.
Ben's grandfather racks the balls
with a sharp click,
as infinitely they circle the table
searching for the perfect shot.

Soon, we too will arrive in another place,
far from home, but unchanged,
singing along with the same dumb country songs
on the car radio. At night the same geese
flying low over another ice-bound lake.

Voices

after "They Feed They Lion," by Philip Levine

Out of the clouds of old shoes,
the deck of love letters
to the dead, that survive,
out of date,
out of dust,
out of long ago dresses in plastic
moth-eaten from the hem up,
as sycamore leaves by frost,
out of wedlock,
out of attics of light
and dark, and broken
box springs and main springs
of a Grandfather clock,
whose face the moon
passed over every night,
we hear voices,
as from the chimney
where swallows hazard a nest,
out of fire and hickory
burned down to ash,
and dusty snapshots
in sepia, brown on white
photos of uncompromised joy.

*

In the attic the seaman's trunk
mouldering green. How different
from the collapsed remains
of our bodies stored underground,
with no steps of memory,

no years of silence stacked overhead.
Out of ancient catalogues
of forgotten varieties
of garden tomatoes,
we hear voices,
out of sample packs of seeds,
the wheeze of an old woman
who never poked down
forefinger-deep
these pumpkin squash,
dug canals for lettuce
and spinach seed, out of the bloom
of the ascendance from spade
and manure and the same
raw sunlight as today.
Out of the attic we drag down voices,
out of boredom,
out of drizzling spring rain:
the click of porcelain tea cups,
the creak of weakened beams,
the resurrection of the body,
the life everlasting,
from trunk to trunk, amen.

Part
II

Desire

From a hundred yards you begin
that achingly slow migration to burn
at my feet, while I lay
barbed-wire
through climax forest of hardwood and ash,
guiding this fence through blackberry
bramble and spring slurred stream,
clear-cutting
sixty-year-old blackjack, burr oak, southern red,
chipping corner posts through topsoil
of rocks scattered, like first rain shaken
from the wind. Living without me
so long, you climb the fence posts left behind.
Black, mute tick
of pure longing, aching to touch
my own ache tucked deep inside.
Back you crawl,
by the end of lunch, from the muck
where I have thrown you, unbroken
peck of midnight in the first full light of spring. Too late,
you return this time and bury
your face in the red cedar post still
fresh with the lingering hot breath of my hands.

Starlings

Who has left them here to blacken the trees,
Even in winter, these cheap violins
Scraping December fugues on oily wings.

All night they have clouded the oak limbs
Until they rise together, in stuttering flight,
A thousand grey hyphens at dawn.

From the dark harvest of glare ice and pinnacle ice,
The frozen clots of field, they will never leave
Waiting out spring with a few bitter juncos and jays.

They are the only friends to Carl, who feeds them
Stolen lunch scraps from his dormer window—
Ham sandwich husk and apple core.

Each day he rides the city bus in Green Bay Packer's ski cap,
And chipped glasses, east to the town of Rising Sun,
Where his starlings have gathered in sumac and hollyhock

To welcome him, like the high school brass band
Playing George Cohan as he shuffled home from Sicily,
Through snow crusts of a second World War.

Later, after smoking a second pack of Luckys
And checking the post office for junk mail, he waves on
His cloud of birds trailing the bus's diesel plume.

He imagines, a million starlings shrouding the state,
A black canopy cracking limbs and lifting
At sunrise with the ice mist from crushed fields,

And always these friends he wakes to at dawn, *Looney, Short
Deck, Fly South*, circling the frost glazed windows of his room,
like tiny metal filings dancing the tarantela inside his brain.

Crows

And once, when I was strolling in the woods I decided
that when we die, we all return as crows.

Stephen Dobyns

From the front fenders of Cadillacs,
they rise over Polk County, then settle
back to their splintered meals
of road-kill skunk and squirrel.
Bored with rocking on power lines
they call you to come out of your room.
They want company, they want
to laugh at you, shambling slowly
over the brown rasp of lawn.
Tonight, when you wake, after midnight,
and walk north of the house, crossing
the barbed wire, to where a flock
of crows pick corn droppings
slipped from the harvester's brittle fingers,
no one will ask you to leave.
No one will notice you flying,
like smoke, through the trees,
as if you too had risen,
raw as November, from the black
clap of bare fields. All your wishes
plowed under, the way crows
clean the last shattered husk
of opposum from the road,
the way they return at midnight
to this cold black earth, because
it reminds them there is nowhere else to go.

Carp and Drum

Through shallows they rise
glistening in sun, wiggling
in mud, sucking air,
fifty carp and drum fanning
their black dorsel fins.
They fall to flap on one side,
as three, now six kids,
with nets and seines,
swarm the pool
more fish than water.
On the pedestrian bridge,
a young man leans
over the rail, arms stretched out,
as if to collect
and raise up
these rough fish,
black as powder burns,
that even the egrets won't eat.
As a child, the fish I caught
I could not clean, lift out
guts, yellow egg stream.
And when the hook settled
far down the tearing
free was like some newfound
knowledge, inevitable
as sleep. When I leave,
he is still there,
sucking the same hot summer air
as thrashing children
and dazed carp risen
from water to the new world,
come out on land
with no feet, just a fin
to slap and slap like a broken wing.

Arkansas River

From Colorado east through the immense
desolation of southern Kansas,
the Arkansas, dark as Karo Syrup,
tangles its slow S curve
through Tulsa, then on through the outskirts
of small towns, each with its own bridge
vaulting the river: Jenks,
Sand Springs, Bixby, Coweta, Gore,
and at the end the Mississippi
and its roiling mud-thick scrawl.

Over the bank someone has rolled
a shopping cart. Listing on its side
it collects nothing but cast up
bones of wind and water.
The great carp, rocking along the bottom,
swim inside the latticed ribs.
Under the bridge old men gather
like fish at the river's edge.
When one falls in, dragged down
by cheap port, no one will remember.
He was only human, and he slept in the river.

Reincarnation in the Heartland

They will be remembered
for the living blood
goring the slaughter shed,
numbered for curing
fatback, for counting
by haunches and loins.
When asked, they will
have no higher math
to account for killing
Hampshires and China Whites,
slowed with autumn sun.
For those who lived
with polished cleavers
in their raised hands,
to return again,
to set foot again
on this ripe green prairie
must seem some infinite
pleasure—to kick up
their trotters and squeal,
to remember nothing
but the God-given
love of sludge and mud.

Iowa Winter

The gray sticks of wind pull up stakes,
and nothing lies down for long.
North of Kansas and here—
nearly Nebraska—winter leans close
in the night, pawing at the screen.

Spectres of snow, orphaned of earth
and air, blow back and forth for days
nuzzling beneath the front porch,
with dogs and cats bundled together,
like old coats stuffed under the door.

Through the months of ancient names,
December and February, and in between
January with its calendar of new days,
and rising mounds of hard pack
in the Safeway parking lots,

snow's white seed overruns the cornfield,
the garden, finally even the snowfence
goes under, with lug nuts
and basketballs, wading through
a darker world until spring.

At midnight we go out to shovel.
In Iowa winter there are only collective
memories: for houses, the clouds of oak
and hickory raising their flag of shelter.
Our shovels remember, digging in on the long drive.

And looking up we are not surprised
by the tug of another gravity raising us,
great coated, through the steam
of our straining breath,
through new fields of falling snow.

Homecoming

for Chris

In the black bare ground of pig-lots, in meat-markets,
and truck stops—where waitresses still sing
Loretta Lynn, in the fractured narrative of isolate houses,

on the dusty roads off County Line—
nothing has changed,
but you kneeling down to the locking-in till spring.

Returning to Iowa, through the unremarkable miles
of corn silk in September, settling in this town,
where each house still unfolds its old assurances.

It is all expected, even after thirty years, the son
comes home to the heavy shoes of autumn, and corn
like a privacy fence, or the desire for silence on three sides.

Out front on the dirt road you memorize
an endless procession of combines and planters,
raising your hand, palm up, as if expecting rain.

First Church of the Open Bible, Tulsa, Oklahoma, 1965

I cannot tell you how we arrived
in that place, on Sunday
morning, with black winged
ceiling fans pushing around bad air.
These were not familiar
hymns and the singers
seemed to break their voices,
over the high notes,
like hard, day labor.
Most of all I remember,
the preacher and another man
climbing a ladder to the silvered
tank of clear water, and
lowering themselves inside,
as the congregation peered
through double-paned glass—
the way I'd watched
angel fish at the pet store,
or half-wit polar bears
at the zoo; and how
the third time this man was dragged
under, he gazed out
from his new, back-lit kingdom
and almost waved, I imagined,
his stiff brown hair rising
a little, as if lifting out of his head.

Mantle—Late August, 1967

for Gary and Glenn

If I took your name then, in the back yard,
with Davey Green
throwing Bunning's slider hard at the knees,
and if with plastic bat
I caught one and lifted another out of the yard,
crossing the street,
and over the barbed wire where longhorns
grazed, and even Mays
could not bring that one back, it was all
for you Mick,
a summer's lost tennis balls, marigolds, settled
in the close cropped pastures.
In Coweta, or Henryetta your bad knees
didn't matter,
at least not at the plate and to 50,000 sweat red fans
in Yankee Stadium
where everyone believed, somehow in the swing,
the stunned
flight, when the crowd knew, in sweet crack,
how the ball
would settle, bounce twice and settle, into reaching hands,
while I counted
the homers left, the ones to follow over
the outfield wall.
Through the heat of summer, I practiced
lonely piano scales
by the screen door waiting to collect the news,
the box scores,
Mantle: one for four, but a homer, and imagined
how you watched
maybe the last one rise safely over Fenway.
At evening practice

I misjudged little league grounders, wearing
your number 7,—
and slept weary in the cool pull of attic fan,
as the Yanks
droned on under the pillow. It was better
that way,
to understand early how Maris hit 61,—while you
went down in pain.
Maybe, if baseball was less complex than a failing marriage,
I would not care
how in mid-March's cold showers, the trees raise
first green buds,
while in Florida on creaking knees the Yanks
carry on without you.
Now at thirty, I rise in the morning,
on knees still stiff
with rain, for the box scores: summer's obsession
of double headers
in minor league parks from Charlotte, to Broken Bow,
to Tulsa,
and once a year, raise a bat from the hall closet,
and stepping
to the plate, swing from the heels, and limp
around third
and slide home for good measure, for you, Mick,
for twenty years of missing you.

Obsession: Elegy for Roger Maris and Georgia O'Keeffe

If I were Georgia O'Keeffe, in last light,
when every cow's skull rises
from its tangle of sage and the ragged night's edge,
I would paint, bone white,
the eternity of a long ball
reaching over the right-field fence,
whose one perfect word the crowd
roar carries through the faltering dark,
through New York, through 1961.

Over Yankee Stadium, I would paint
one more home run, the last
of that long season of '61,
above a landscape of blue shirt sleeves.
And outside the frame, Maris
would remain, in every bone and ganglion
alone at home plate, the cock-sure
knowing that finally he'd got it right.

In New Mexico, the sun sets over mule deer
come down from the hills,
like invisible Piute women
shaking out fresh linen at midday,
while a lone woman kicks up dust devils
walking home at dusk from painting
in the back seat of a rusting Model A.

Over these ancient peaks of sand
and rock worn down to bone,
the North Star comes clear,
first light in an azure sky,

like a single baseball hanging so long
we have all stopped cheering,
for thirty years, just stopped
to watch, as no one
will ever bring that one back.

The Legend of Kingman Boulevard, After Hours

Long after the night settles
its sentimental glove
over all the ignorance on Kingman Boulevard,
and the late shift has released us
to this street, where no one mistakes
Freddie's grocery or Payless Liquors
for the estates of fond memories,

we come home, to clouds of cicadas,
and the nightly blues of Coltrane
and Ellington sweeping through this street,
like heat lightning from The Legendary
After All Hours Bar.

Here, in the dead of summer
nothing speaks, but the thud of June bugs
all night asking their way in. But now,
every young couple on the block
has turned their TV down,
as an old jazz man blows his nightly vigil
all the way to the perfect lawns of Lexington Avenue.

Imagine this, just another night,
imagine love in this neighborhood—
the backrooms at the Legend, and those women
with voices of angora. For Carl Brown,
proprietor, there was only one miracle—
to live on without sleep:
hauling ladders of a window service
to Iowa Parcel, and boxes of weariness
back after midnight to his third floor bar.

Tonight, as I lay down after hours,
after even the Legend has closed,
and the sun is inching its slow ass
out of the Raccoon River,
I understand how weariness
carried on so long
may give way to the rough-tongued
tenderness of this summer's night.

The All-Night Diner

Tonight, you will not tire
of waitresses with free refills.
The eggs you ordered a decade ago
may never appear. It doesn't matter.
In the next booth, James Dean
punches the jukebox on the wall,
and whispers in your ear, "no one returns
from the all-night diner,"
and you believe him.
The selection is endless,
and eternity begins with "Teen Angel,"
then "Dead Man's Curve." In back,
a medley of sunburned tourists,
just off the boat to paradise,
select Don Ho melodies
and piña coladas, or coffee
with miniature cows for cream.
Patience is not a virtue here,
but a way of watching
the waitresses in their slow
unhurried gate. They have been here
since the beginning and know
just how to walk without
bumping the stools,
or even lying down to sleep
on marbled counters, or wondering
when the pale moon will finally
rise off the front glass
to take its place in the neon firmament,
as someone pulls the shades
and turns over the vacancy sign to full.

PART III

The Kindness of Strangers

Apples, Nick calls them,
achingly red, these cherries,
his prize for turning two.
Already, he has stripped
the lowest branches and now wades
patiently over the back patio
hollering at the flocks
of robins to release
the cherries they have claimed.
Today, earthworms swim safely
under the back lawn
and the grey fledglings
in their nest are stained
crimson with their parents' desire.
When I look back, Nick is eating
again, ripe fruits picked
and fumbled by the birds,
or perhaps tossed down to him
waiting below, mouth open,
trusting to fate, in grace,
in the kindness of strangers.

Gabriel at Eighteen Months

Now we are his to comfort and hold,
Inert polar caps of love he navigates between,
Pulling arm hairs, counting teeth,
Caressing lips, noses, sleep's dark tangle
Of hair still clinging to the pillows.

In this world of Gabe, only he is free
From the slow anthem of dreams we hum
Together. Delighted, he squeals for our cat yawning
At the foot of the bed, tossing all his favored words
Into the dark, "hot dog, mama, shoot-ball."

Soon we too will wake to the reality
Of breakfast at 5 a.m., peeling away blankets,
Tottering off to the kitchen, to sometimes wonder,
Over coffee and Gerbers Rice Cereal,
What language could ever replace this touch,

This vocabulary of Gabe at eighteen months,
  Our hair gone dumb,
    Our ears untouched,
      Our noses forever unloved,
        Our lips sealed with sleep.

This Miracle Was Meant for Her Alone

And all the miracles that have not yet healed in me.
Yehuda Amichai

Tonight, we are wasting time
in a laundromat. My four-year-old draws
as I lean over this legal pad.
From thick smears of color, her figures
appear dancing on nothingness,
like the guardian angels of Marc Chagall,
who were common as houseflies.
Beside me, Laurel piles landscapes,
portraits, still life with flying washing machine,
while I search for a few perfect words.
It was Chagall who delivered us
from a reasonable world
to the comfort of wings, or lovers ascending
in the stunned light of midday.
This time, when I ask for an angel,
Laurel brings one red bird, great
as the kingdom of heaven, waving
long-fingered wings over a sleeping town.
Below a single child waits,
pushing her face to the kitchen window.
This miracle was meant for her alone.

Starlings, Grackles, Redwings

Someday, in someone else's dark future,
They will arrive in distant trees
Filling the yards for blocks around
With their lunatic blackbird cries.

But this morning in our pines
These late summer carolers have stopped over.
Laurel, rising early for her first day
Of school, wakes us to six peering in
The bedroom window. She is delighted
And hauls the cat off the bed,
Who, just waking too, decides this must be Christmas.

In another town thousands have settled
In the city park. The neighbors are horrified.
Weeks later the men will discard
Their shotguns and settle down to wait,
As dead blackbirds mean less than empty shells.

How do I explain to my daughter
That these birds are not beautiful,
Like cottonwoods, or Grandmother's
Peonnies which rely on ants to open
Their garish pink buds? How many springs
Will we find cropped dandelions
On the mantle, in the cat's bowl,
Like the best gift this earth has given?

Skating by Ice House Light

At eight, Laurel still knows God loves her,
here on the ice, where deer have crossed
in the night, just hours before.
They are blessed as my daughter,
for whom Christmas still arrives suddenly,
through the hard pack of winter
to uncover distant family
and ice skates curled under the tree.

Tonight, idling our old white Chevy
off Lake Side Drive, we will wait
together for the first lights,
Coleman Lanterns like late December
fireflies hovering over the lake,
collecting at the deepest pools
where thirty pound muskies,
in half-sleep, graze black water.

She would like to go out skating,
crossing the lake by ice house light,
stopping at each shack to sign "Laurel,"
in perfect figure eights—
a trail of bread crumbs, she imagines,
to guide her back whenever she desires.
And inside, the fishermen who wonder
if the steelheads will ever strike.

Thirteen-Year Cicadas

Another night collects under the streetlights
lit too soon, while this summer's herald,
cicadas, rising once every thirteen years,
have returned to the comatose world beneath
the lawn. Now, only a few crickets are left
to answer the autumn call of last leaves
browned and aching for the wind to release
them to the wind. This is the hour of night
my children know nothing about.
When I tuck them down into the deep grass
of sleep, they are restless, returning for a cup
of water, or one last flicker of moonlight
peering through the door. Finally they are satisfied,
the radio sweeping Pachelbel under the bed,
filling the empty corners of their room.
At midnight I rush back inside to carry
my daughter out for the best meteor shower
of the year. Look, there in Pleiades I say,
as another bright seam tears open the sky.
But only for a few moments can she brush back
the thick pre-adolescent sleep.
At nine, she knows nothing is lost—she is not waiting,
for winter to pardon the bare lawn
with snow, for the leaves to remember
again in spring, the livid green of leaves.
The morning, she knows, will never wake
without her, and the night will return again
tomorrow, and when she is twenty-two,
as she steps outside into early June, to the tune
of thirteen-year cicadas returned
to their trees. Overhead, shooting stars
through the Northern Cross as she remembers them,
once before, breaking loose from sleep.

Collecting the Light

Each night of this summer my children collect
fireflies from the cusp of darkness,
impatient for the first, waking always
over a neighbor's yard. With each catch
they race inside to show me, lights out,
the green radiance seeping through fingers.

On the bedroom wall, they have assembled
florescent constellations—her Pleiades, his Cygnus—
from nights charting the sky on the back lawn.
While stars outside shower the window
with small cold buckets of light,
their plastic neon beacons burn
for ten borrowed minutes overhead.

In bed, after the last wall star has crawled
back into its night skin, my children
find no comfort lingering in their small tight fists,
as new galaxies rise from the ditch
between our yard and the road—
a corona of fireflies—coalescing
in Queen Anne's Lace, Nightshade and Goldenrod.

When I return to pat their covers, and await
the ebb tide of night breath, I find six,
maybe ten, fireflies drifting in and out the empty window,
like guardian angels who, I want to believe,
collect above these beds at dusk, waving
green silk lanterns, all night, after I am gone.

Markham Johnson is executive director of the Associated Writing Programs at Old Dominion University. He grew up in Tulsa, Oklahoma, attended Eckerd College in St. Petersburg, Florida, and earned an M.F.A. in creative writing from Vermont College. He has taught creative writing at Drake University and Simpson College and has served as executive director of the Michigan Festival. His poems have appeared widely in literary journals, and a chapbook, *Starlings, Grackles, Redwings,* was published in 1991 by *South Florida Poetry Review.* He lives in Virginia Beach, Virginia, with his wife and three children.

University of Central Florida Contemporary Poetry Series

Diane Averill, *Branches Doubled Over with Fruit*
George Bogin, *In a Surf of Strangers*
Van K. Brock, *The Hard Essential Landscape*
Jean Burden, *Taking Light from Each Other*
Lynn Butler, *Planting the Voice*
Daryl Ngee Chinn, *Soft Parts of the Back*
Robert Cooperman, *In the Household of Percy Bysshe Shelley*
Rebecca McClanahan Devet, *Mother Tongue*
Rebecca McClanahan Devet, *Mrs. Houdini*
Gerald Duff, *Calling Collect*
Malcolm Glass, *Bone Love*
Barbara L. Greenberg, *The Never-Not Sonnets*
Susan Hartman, *Dumb Show*
Lola Haskins, *Forty-four Ambitions for the Piano*
Lola Haskins, *Planting the Children*
William Hathaway, *Churlsgrace*
William Hathaway, *Looking into the Heart of Light*
Michael Hettich, *A Small Boat*
Roald Hoffmann, *Gaps and Verges*
Roald Hoffmann, *The Metamict State*
Greg Johnson, *Aid and Comfort*
Markham Johnson, *Collecting the Light*
Hannah Kahn, *Time, Wait*
Michael McFee, *Plain Air*
Richard Michelson, *Tap Dancing for the Relatives*
Judith Minty, *Dancing the Fault*
David Posner, *The Sandpipers*
Nicholas Rinaldi, *We Have Lost Our Fathers*
CarolAnn Russell, *The Red Envelope*
Robert Siegel, *In a Pig's Eye*
Edmund Skellings, *Face Value*
Edmund Skellings, *Heart Attacks*
Ron Smith, *Running Again in Hollywood Cemetery*
Katherine Soniat, *Cracking Eggs*
Don Stap, *Letter at the End of Winter*